# GOD'S REPOSITIONED MAN

## BY
## MIKE BROWN

First Edition

First Printing • 1,000 • November 1995

ISBN 1-57502-079-3

Printed in the USA by

*M*ORRIS
PUBLISHING

3212 E. Hwy 30
Kearney, NE 68847
800-650-7888

# Contents

Dedication

Acknowledgements

Preface

Introduction

# Chapters

# Dedication

*This book
is dedicated to
the loving memory of my grandmother,
the late Corrine Lilly Johnson.
I regret that you never had
the opportunity to see the development
of your number three grandson.
I'm a senior pastor now because you
prayed me into the Kingdom of God.
Thank you for loving me
through my troubled
rebellious years.*

# Acknowledgements

To my Heavenly Father whom I love with all my heart, mind, soul, and strength.

To my lovely wife, Debra Ann, and children. Especially my baby son, Joshua Mikel, who has been my inspiration.

To the Sparkman Family for being so faithful in following the vision God called me to.

To Charles "Charlie" Babers for your reading and editing ability.

To the Christian Joy Center of El Paso, Tx.: Thank you for providing the laboratory, love and support. Your lives have touched me in so many different ways.

# Preface

As you scan the political, economic, and social landscape of our world, one regrettable truth cries out. Something is seriously wrong! As gang violence, starvation, and a myriad of old and new infectious diseases continue to claim thousands of lives each year, it appears that our planet is spinning wildly out of control. Crime continues to escalate unchecked. The abortion industry boasts staggering profits annually as teenage pregnancies continue to climb every year. To further exacerbate our troubled situation, entrusted political leaders continue to steer us into economic ruin by their unconstitutional deficit spending practices. What possible answer can we offer to explain our present condition?

All across this nation men are abdicating their God-given responsibilities at alarming rates. Instead of rising to the occasion and taking control of worsening worldwide social conditions, men have opted to run to the hills for cover, leaving the women and children behind to pick up the broken pieces. As this mass exodus of able bodied men continues to bleed this nation of it's most stabilizing resource, huge cavernous vacuums are being created in every facet of our existence. Consequently, women have had to leave their duties at home to do a man's job. This shift in roles to compensate for the man's failure to assume responsibility has produced a devastating backlash of consequences which have utterly destroyed the moral and social fabric of this entire world. Is there any answer to this perilous situation that is fueled by an ever present absence of responsible men?

**God's Repositioned Man** examines this important issue in detail from a Biblical perspective. It is a poignant commentary on our current state of affairs and seeks to explain how we have arrived at our present predicament. As men continue to operate out of the prescribed roles set by God, our world will continue on its present downhill course. Men cannot delegate their God-ordained responsibilities to the rest of humanity and expect all to be well when they return home. Just as Adam had no right to blame Eve for his decision to bite of the Forbidden Fruit, men, in general, cannot continue to point the finger to explain away our current economic and social conditions.

The best part about this book is that it reveals the hope that does exist for mankind. God is in the process of repositioning men in order to restore them to their original position. As men rediscover God's original purpose for their lives, tremendous potential to effect positive change is released. Society at large benefits immeasurably when men begin to turn their hearts toward God for direction. When this occurs, families begin to operate as designed. Worldwide economies are stimulated as men of integrity steer us toward productive and prosperous new vistas. Furthermore, governments worldwide begin to be responsive to the needs of their citizens as Godly men begin to restore political order. All this will happen when God's repositioned man returns to duty.

**Gary N. Sparkman**

# Introduction

Men are curious and inquisitive creatures. Even from birth, we are constantly seeking new knowledge and novel experiences. We ask questions, and search for answers. Through the centuries, the questions most often asked by men are, "Who am I? Why am I here?" We want to know how we came to be, and what our place is in the universe. Were we an accident of nature, or were we purposely created by One greater than us? Are we here for a particular purpose, or are we bouncing randomly through history without a plan or a destination?

At different times in human history, we have either looked inwardly to find the answers to these questions within ourselves, or looked outwardly to find answers in the things that we can observe and experience through our senses. The ancient Greeks believed that they could understand man's origin and purposes through the power of pure thought, alone. They looked inwardly for their answers. Beginning in about the sixteenth century, mankind experienced an explosion of intellectual development known as the Renaissance. During this period, men came to believe that the way to know and understand anything, including the reasons that we are here, where we came from, and where we are going, was through scientific observation. They looked outwardly— at the way men lived and acted and at the world in which men lived—to try to find their answers. Throughout history, but seemingly more so during this century, men have again turned inwardly to find their answers. Beginning in the 1960s people have used drugs, meditation, hypnotism, sensory deprivation and other means to reach "higher states of consciousness" through which they might find the hidden truths within themselves or the universe.

In this book, Pastor Mike Brown cuts through all the confusion and explains the origin and purposes of man based on God's word, the Bible. Using scriptural examples, he explains how God originally created man for a purpose, how that purpose was subverted by Satan, and how Jesus' death on the cross laid the groundwork for man to be repositioned back to that original purpose. Pastor Brown then explains, in detail, who we are for those of us who call ourselves "children of God". This is must reading for every born again Christian, and a valuable resource for anyone who wants to understand his place in God' s creation. I highly recommend it.

# 1

# God's Repositioned Man

Satan, the father of deception, has a diabolical plan to deceive men and blind them to their true purpose, and he has successfully executed that plan for years. Because his ultimate goal is to keep man from getting close to God, he has a system at work in every race under the sun. He causes men to wander aimlessly in the wilderness seeking approval or validation of their manhood. Satan understands that as men, everything stands and falls on the security that we have in our manhood. We define ourselves, our identities and our self-worth based on a societal ideal of manhood. It is more popular today for men to be "lovers" than it is for them to be real men. It's more popular to gain or seek after the wealth of this world and to pursue a career than it is to be a real man. Real men are men who are first sold out to the purposes of God and the plan that God has for their lives. Real men are not created to find fulfillment in what this world mistakenly calls "love", but which is really irresponsible sex, nor in wealth, careers or the display of physical strength. Real love is more than sex, but is complete and unconditional, and is best illustrated by the love that God the Father showed for man when He gave His Son to die for our sins. Real wealth is not measured in dollars and cents or by a successful career, but in the true riches of the Kingdom of God. Real strength is not that which is outwardly, but that which is inwardly. It is the character of the person. This strength is not given, it is developed.

To understand God's plan to reposition men, we must first understand God's original purpose for man. To do this we need to go back to the beginning--to the creation of the first man. We can then determine how God desired man to live and what his relationship was supposed to be to his partner (the woman), to the earth and all creatures placed upon it, and to God. The best place to begin our examination of God's plan for the repositioned man is in the Bible's book of Genesis.

The first man, whom we know as Adam (meaning man taken from the earth or taken from the red clay), was created both male and female in one body. Gen 1:26-28 says:

God said, "Let us make man in our image, after our likeness, and let them have dominion over the fish of the sea, and over the fowl of the air, and over the cattle, and over all the earth, and over every creeping thing that creepeth upon the earth. So God created man in His own image, in the image of God created He him; male and female created He them. And God blessed them, and God said unto them. Be fruitful, and multiply, and replenish the earth, and subdue it; and have dominion over the fish of the sea, and over the fowl of the air, and over every living thing that moveth upon the earth.

God created male and female within the man. He did not create the flesh as male only, but the spirit He created male. Gen 2:7 says, "And the Lord God formed man of the dust of the ground and breathed into his nostrils the breath of life, and man became a living soul." He breathed into man the essence of life, the soul. Man then became a living, logical, rational human being--a very soul-filled person. So why didn't God create the fleshly woman first? Because God was first establishing the leader, teacher and head of mankind. He established the man because

His purpose was that there first must be a head. He wanted the origin of human life to begin with the man.

Gen 2:18-19 says:

> And the Lord God said, It is not good that the man should be alone; I will make him an help meet for him. And out of the ground the Lord formed every beast of the field, and every fowl of the air; and brought them unto Adam to see what he would call them: and whatsoever Adam called every living creature, that was the name thereof.

Adam was a very intellectual, brilliantly intelligent individual. He used a large percentage of his brain capacity. Some people say that most of us today use only about four to eight percent of our brain. This means that those of us who are using eight percent of our brains are better than most, but still somewhat average. Those who are using twelve percent or more can be considered geniuses. But even those that do use twelve percent or more are yet confined by their mentality. That is why God tells us to walk in the spirit and not in the flesh, so that our potential will be limitless. Adam, however, was a very intellectual person who was able to do many things that we are unable to do today because he had not yet learned to be limited by his flesh. He had the power to choose and select, as he did when he named the animals. Adam exercised dominion over that which God purposed for him to dominate. God brought every animal, two-by-two or one-by-one to Adam who named every single one without any prior knowledge of what to name them. He didn't second-guess or change his mind once he had named something. If he saw a giraffe, he said, "You will be called a 'giraffe'." That is how intellectually brilliant and intelligent Adam was.

Look at the method that God used to develop Adam is his position of leadership. All of the animals were under Adam's control and leadership. Adam was destined to dominate the animals and everything else on the earth, and in the beginning he did. Today, we are not dominating the animals--we live in fear of them. I do not care what anyone says about how many animals are in zoos. They are not under man's dominion. If you doubt it, go into the wild places of this earth and see if you can dominate a lion. You can only dominate them as long as they are behind bars. Adam truly dominated the animals. I am a firm believer that God created us to dominate all animals and not be afraid of them. Man was positioned and God wanted him to dominate everything.

> And Adam gave names to all the cattle and every beast of the field, but for Adam there was not found a help meet for him (Gen 2:20)

Notice that Adam all of a sudden sees, as he is naming all the animals, that each male animal had a counterpart which gave them the capability to reproduce their own kind. We have already determined that Adam was very intelligent. He knew what to do with the male organ that God had given him. God had told him in spirit to be fruitful and multiply and reproduce; however, he did not have a female counterpart to help him for the purpose of reproduction. He had no one.

God had brought the animals to Adam not only for him to name them, but also so that he could see what he was destitute of. He was destitute of a woman. He needed a woman by his side to help him to reproduce, be fruitful and multiply. God had not forgotten that the woman had not yet been created. His intention was to use the man to produce the woman. We must understand that the spirit of the man came from God, but the flesh that produced the woman came from man. "And the Lord God caused a deep sleep to fall upon Adam, and he slept: and He took one of his ribs, and closed up the flesh instead thereof; and the rib, which the Lord God had taken from man, made the woman, and brought her unto the man (Gen 2:21-22). The word "woman" should actually be "womb man" because God made the woman with reproductive equipment (a womb) so that she could carry the man's seed. The seed of all humanity was in the man, not in the woman. The woman is the carrier of the seed. She brings the seed forward and develops it within her female organs. Once the seed is planted within her from the male, it implants itself inside the egg and produces a male or female child as God has destined it to be. Even the rib that God used to create the woman (Eve) was a type of seed. You see, all of human life came from man, not from woman. Adam was the father of all life--even of Eve. After Eve came forth and bore the first son, she became the mother of all life that came after, but she was not the original mother of all life. Adam was both the original father and mother of all life.

In Gen 2:23 we read, "And Adam said, This is now bone of my bones, and flesh of my flesh: she shall be called Woman, because she was taken out of Man". I often hear women saying that men ought to thank their mothers for giving them life. We should love our mothers, but we originally came from man, not woman. If there had been no Adam, there would have been no seed with which to produce the woman. [Glory to God! Amen!] God began to do something very important with Adam and this seed, the rib that He took out of humanity to make the woman. If we look back at the latter part of Gen 2:22, we read that after God had made the woman, He brought her to Adam. Notice an interesting thing that happens here. In the 19th verse God brought the animals to Adam. In verse 22, He brought the newly created woman to Adam as well. But God was doing something totally different there, because Adam knew that the woman was a person that he was not to dominate, but to lead. He knew it intellectually and instinctively. He knew from the very beginning that God had created someone equal to him in intellect. You can not dominate your own kind, your equals. God brought the woman to Adam, not to dominate, but to lead and to teach. Adam became the teacher because God gave all the instruction and information to him first. He was in turn to teach it to Eve.

Adam was the first man. He exercised dominion over the animals effectively. He used his intellect wisely; however, his real challenge laid ahead in exercising leadership. Even today, man's challenge is not in teaching his dog to roll over and play dead, it is in leading his family. This new woman whom God had created was made Adam's equal in most respects. Adam knew that the woman was equal to him in intelligence and had a mind of her own. As the man, Adam now had to lead the woman who was his equal in intellect but weaker than him in physical strength. His responsibility was to teach her what God had taught him, because he was ordained to be the teacher.

So what did God teach Adam that he was to teach his wife? In Gen 2:15 we read that, "...the Lord God took the man, and put him into the garden of Eden to dress it and to keep it". This was one of the first lessons that Adam was taught, the first position of responsibility in which he was placed. He was placed in the position of taking care of, training, nurturing and beautifying the garden. God was teaching him how to take care of his own, to protect his own.

Adam learned and developed those skills right there in the garden. He was placed in this position, and taught the lesson of responsibility before Eve was on the scene. In the 16th verse God commanded him, "...of every tree of the garden thou mayest freely eat: But of the tree of the knowledge of good and evil thou shalt not eat of it; for in the day that thou eatest thereof thou shalt surely die." Adam was taught this lesson by God. He and God exchanged dialog. They had an intimate personal relationship, communion, fellowship and conversation with one another. That is why men long to be close to their creator—because that is what we once had with God. God originally taught Adam, He fellowshipped with Adam, and they talked face to face. They were friends. God was the only being with whom Adam could verbally communicate. However, Adam was not on the same level with God, so there was something missing from his existence. Then God created Eve as his mate, helper and partner. So God taught Adam everything that he needed to know and everything that he was to teach Eve. And Adam did teach Eve, his wife. He taught her just what God had first taught him. Eventually, however, we will see how what he had taught her was turned around and used against him. It is funny that so often the thing that you are taught is the very thing that is used to challenge you.

Now the serpent was more subtil than any beast of the field which the Lord God had made. And he said unto the woman [this is Satan speaking through the serpent], "Yea, hath God said, Ye shall not eat of every tree of the garden? And the woman said unto the serpent, we may eat of the fruit of the trees of the garden: But of the fruit of the tree which is in the midst of the garden: God hath said, Ye shall not eat of it, neither shall ye touch it, lest ye die (Gen 3:1-3)

If we examine her statement, we will see that she has added to her teaching something that she was never taught. God never taught Adam that he could not touch the tree, nor did Adam teach this to Eve. God said nothing about touching it. Adam had the ability, if he wanted, to destroy the tree and nothing would have happened to him. God taught him to subdue, conquer and rule, and that included the trees as well as the animals. He taught Eve all the things that she needed to know, what she should not do and what she should. She then turns around and adds onto what she has been taught. The next verses, Gen 3:4-6 say:

> And the serpent said unto the woman, Ye shall not surely die: for God doth know that in the day ye eat thereof, then your eyes shall be opened, and ye shall be as gods, knowing good and evil. And when the woman saw that the tree was good for food, and this it was pleasant to the eyes, and a tree to be desired to make one wise, she took of the fruit thereof, and did eat, and gave also unto her husband with her; and he did eat.

Where was Adam while the serpent was deceiving Eve? He was with her. Instead of protecting her, he was standing beside her listening to the conversation. He let her do what he did not want her to do. He should have just pulled her away and ordered the serpent to leave or he would kill it. He had the right to tell the serpent what to do because God had given him dominion over all the animals. He had every right to literally kill the serpent. He could not kill Satan, but he could have killed the serpent, since Satan was just using the serpent's body. It was very clear to Adam that he was to dominate, but all of a sudden, he is not dominating. He is not taking control. There is a problem here. This same problem that occurred with Adam is still occurring today. Men are not accepting their responsibility. Adam had every legal right to take control of the situation. Even though he was not to dominate his wife, he was to lead her. He could have said, "Woman, leave that serpent alone!" Instead, he listens to the conversation, knowing the truth but does not say anything. There is a term for what Adam did. It is called tacit approval (tacit meaning "silent"). When we see something happening that we know is wrong, but we say nothing about it or do nothing to stop it, we are giving our tacit approval of what is happening. This is what happens today. Wives come in saying things "off the top of their heads", and men are too intimidated to say anything. Instead of taking control and saying "Woman, you're talking like a foolish woman, That's not right! " Men just say to themselves, "Well, I'm just going to leave her alone and let her get over it." This is wrong. Job told his wife that she talked like a foolish woman. We need to have the strength to do the same thing. There is one fact that no one can ever deny: the female needs the strength and leadership of the male.

The male needs to understand that he is in the position to dominate. Where his family goes or does not go is his responsibility as he leads them. Satan was in Adam's domain - where Adam was supposed to be the dominator, but it was Satan, not Adam who was dominating the situation. It is sad that we will allow people to come into our homes and do whatever they want to do without us saying anything. How can you complain about something that you tolerate? This is what is happening to the man today. He tolerates something and then walks about complaining about it.

Some men get fidgety and nervous around women. When the woman gets a little upset, the man starts giving her whatever she wants, whatever she says, bowing to her every wish and whim, even though he knows that it is selfishness that is controlling her. Men fail to exercise leadership. Adam failed to successfully lead his family. Eve would have followed his leadership because she knew that he was the head, but he would not lead. Maybe Adam had in his mind that she had a mind of her own, so instead of forcefully enforcing the rules that God had given him and possibly getting her upset, he was timid. He could have suggested, "Let me just help you a little bit. Let me influence you a little. Just stay away from that which is evil, which we know will destroy you. Let me take you away from that, please." Adam had a problem here. Because he failed to lead, we see in Gen 3:6 what happened, Eve ate of the fruit of the forbidden tree and gave some of it to Adam. In the seventh verse it says, "And the eyes of them both were opened, and they knew that they were naked," This nakedness that they became aware of was not a physical nakedness. It was a spiritual nakedness. It was a loss of identity. It was a loss of covering. Adam did not only lose his covering (God), but Eve lost hers, because the covering for the woman is the man. Eve lost her covering because Adam did not operate in the position that God had placed him in. I talk to women all the time, and most of them want their husbands to be strong. They want their husbands to take charge. I do not care how much some women try to fight against it, they would be so appreciative if their husbands did not put up with some of their stuff. [Now, some women know that they put their husbands through a lot. I think that it is time for these women to repent. It is hard to lead women when they do not want to follow. You can not lead someone who does not want to be led.]

If man is supposed to be the head, teacher and leader of his family, not the supervisor, the boss nor the dominator, then why are men always turning to their wives and saying, "Baby, can you show me what this means", or "Pray for me, honey"? Why don't the men pray for themselves? Why do men not get into the Word for themselves and find out what this or that means? Because the men of today are lost. They are out of position. They have no identity. Look at our young men today. They are walking around with a chip on their shoulders, trying to prove who they are. We have older men, younger men and middle aged men all trying to prove how manly they are, when they are not. To shoot someone with a gun does not prove how manly you are. To beat up your wife does not show how much of a man you are.

Going back to the book of Genesis, we see that the woman lost the covering of her husband. It was not her fault, even though she was the one who brought him the fruit to eat. It was Adam's fault. God held Adam responsible.

> And they heard the voice of the Lord God walking in the garden in the cool of the day: and Adam and his wife hid themselves from the presence of the Lord God amongst the trees of the garden. And the Lord God called unto Adam, and said unto him, Where art thou? (Gen 3:8-9)

God called out to Adam to show himself. It was not that God did not know where Adam was. What God was saying here is, "I'm not covering you any longer, Adam. You've left your covering. Where are you, Adam? I know where you are physically, but where are you spiritually?" To this Adam answered, "I heard You in the garden, and I was afraid because I was naked, so I hid myself." The first thing that God probably thought was, "Who taught you fear? Who taught you to be embarrassed? Everything was perfect for you.. You had everything. Why did you compromise yourself for the sake of keeping something that I had given you. Adam said "I was afraid because I was naked and I hid myself." [This was the first record of a sin consciousness].

> And He said, Who told thee that thou wast naked? Hast thou eaten of the tree, whereof I commanded thee that thou shouldest not eat? And the man said, The woman whom Thou gavest to be with me, she gave me of the tree, and I did eat. (Gen 3:11-12)

This is really serious. This is no laughing matter, because it is what we still see today. This is why men are so out of position. Instead of leading, Adam was led. He knew what was right, and he knew what was wrong. So the responsibility was on him. He was the teacher, the head and the leader. God meant for him to teach and lead Eve. But all of a sudden, Eve gives unto Adam that which they both knew was wrong, and Adam, like an idiot, takes and eats it. Do you know that we could still have been saved up to this point. Even if Eve did eat of the fruit, man could have been saved and spared, if he had refused to follow her into sin. Eve would have been kicked out of the garden, but Adam would have still been in God's good graces.

Who did God go to once the sin was committed? He did not go to Eve. He went to Adam, because Adam was supposed to be in charge. Because of this first sin, the entire earthly system was changed. God put "Operation Crisis" into action. He began to dole out retribution for the sins that were committed. God says:

> I will put enmity between thee and the woman and between thy seed and her seed; it shall bruise thy head, and thou shalt bruise his heel. Unto the woman

He said, I will greatly multiply thy sorrow
and thy conception; in sorrow thou shalt
bring forth children; and thy desire shall
be to thy husband, and he shall rule over
thee. (Gen 3;15-16)

Do you know why God said it this way and why
He used these terms? It is because man now has no
consciousness of who he is. He has no identity. He
now thinks that everything that is weaker than him,
ought to be dominated. We have so much conflict
and so much abuse in the family today because man
thinks that if he can physically overpower the other
family members, then he can dominate them. That
is the mentality now--survival of the fittest. It is all
because of Adam's falling. Husbands now dominate
their wives because of the curse placed upon Adam.
Man now thinks that anything that is physically
weaker than he is meant to be dominated.

In Gen 3:17 we read:

And unto Adam He said, Because thou
has hearkened unto the voice of thy wife,
and hast eaten of the tree, of which I
commanded thee, saying, Thou shalt not
eat of it; cursed is the ground for thy
sake; in sorrow shalt thou eat of it all the
days of thy life.

Now, God isn't saying that a man shouldn't listen to his wife. Your wife may have some very good things to say. But when the truth is presented by the man, brothers, women are not in a position to dispute that truth. When the truth is disputed and not received, you should just back off and say, "The fact that you are my wife is not why I stand with you; I stand with you because of the truth."

God's curse is now initiated, not because of the woman, but because of the man. The man has failed in his God ordained role as leader, teacher and head. Malachi 4:5 says, "The curse has come." Our families are cursed, our children are cursed and everywhere we go is cursed. Man is out of position. Only when man is repositioned by God is everything blessed. The rest of Malachi 4:6 says "Behold, I will send you Elijah, the prophet, before the coming of the great and dreadful day of the Lord. And he shall turn the hearts of the fathers to the children and the hearts of the children to the fathers, lest I come and smite the earth with a curse." Why is the earth cursed today? Because the hearts of the children are not turned to their fathers, and the hearts of the fathers are not turned to their children. Fathers are out of position. Men are out of position. They are spiritually in the wilderness. They are lost. They do not know where they belong or where their identity comes from. You see, you get your identity from your covering. Identity does not come from the woman, it comes from the man. That is why for years, I myself, wondered who my father was. What did he look like? What color eyes did he have? It was because my identity came from my father. Even this world system says that who and what you are is based on who and what your father was. If your father was Black, that is what you are. If your father was White, then you are White. It makes no difference what your mother was. Everything hinges on the father. It has nothing to do with women, and everything to do with men. The earth is cursed, families are cursed and children are cursed because men are out of position.

The unregenerated man is still looking for his true position. That is why today's man has such a drive to "get somewhere" in life. He is looking for position, for accreditation and for approval. Unfortunately, sometimes the only approval that he can get is from subjugating women, including his wife, his mother, his sister or his daughters. The only accreditation of his self-worth is in using his strength to abuse women, either physically or verbally. So he gets all of his accreditation by putting his wife or any woman down. This is not how it should be. As a man, you are supposed to get all of your accreditation from your creator. God is your covering. When you are with Him, He positions you. He repositions you in your family, in your relationship towards women, in your relationship towards other men and in your relationship with Him. Only when He has repositioned you is God pleased with you, and only then will He come in and commune with you one-on-one.

There is a song that used to be sung years ago. It used to say, "Too many lovers, not enough men today." The words are as true today as they were then, if not more so. Everybody wants to be a "lover"; everybody wants to be a "player". But few want to make the effort to be real men. When men reach a certain age, they are looking for accreditation and approval. It is easy to gain that approval in the eyes of other men. All that is required is to do those things that other men do, say the things that other men say and act the way that other men act. This is why so many men place so much emphasis on how they look, what they own, where they work or who they know. These are the things that the world has told them to define whether or not they have "made it" and whether or not they have "got it". <u>Wake up, men!</u> If you do not get it from God, you are going to keep looking for it. That is why I do not put my stock in my own performance or in what people say about me, because they will curse me one moment and bless me the next. Instead of putting my stock in what people say, I put my stock in everything that God says that I am. I can not afford to listen to people, because then I will stand or fall based on them and what they think or say about me. I have to listen, instead, to God. What is God saying that I am? He says that I am more than a conqueror through Him who loves me! I am a man. I am a man, not because Martin Luther King, Jr. says that I am a man; not because Jesse Jackson says I am, a man. I am a man because I know God intimately, I know Him personally, and I have fellowship in my heart with all three members of the Godhead. I am a man because of Him.

If you notice, in the King James version of the Bible, the word "human" is never used, because as far as God is concerned, He is not dealing with "humanity", He is dealing with man. Humanity is a manly, physical, scientific word. It is a word that man created. But "man" is a word that God created. God created only one type of man, and that man was wholly without sin. What mankind has degenerated into and what we, ourselves, may degenerate into is our own fault. For example, when God brought the animals to Adam and he noticed that each one had a mate, Adam could have said, "Wait a minute...maybe I am supposed to reproduce with one of them!" This is not; however, the reason that the animals were brought to him. It was not what God intended to happen. If it had happened, it would have been the man's fault, not God's.

Man has lost his morals. He does not know what is good, what is right, what is clean and what is not. He does not know how to lead his family or raise his children. Many father children (in or out of wedlock) and figure that they have no more responsibilities towards the lives that they have created--that it is the mother's job to raise her children. Some of those fathers who do participate in the raising of their children tend to ignore their daughters. They consider it their jobs to "make men" out of their sons by teaching their sons to act and think just like they do. They smoke, drink and take drugs in front of their sons and tell them that real men can handle it. So naturally their sons imitate their self-destructive behavior. They teach their sons that women are to be lusted after and desired physically, showing them pictures of naked women in magazines, allowing them to watch x rated movies, taking them to topless or all nude clubs when they come of age, and even by taking them to prostitutes to learn about sex. Through this the enemy (the Devil) is planting the seeds of rape into the minds of our young men. All because some fathers say, "I'm going to make a man out of you." But they are not. Little do they know that they are creating monsters without any moral values. They are developing men who will sneak into the rooms of their children at night and violate their own children or step-children. They are developing men who will have sex with either men or women, young boys or young girls.

There are too many men today who are falling short of the mark. In most cases, the primary reason is that as they were growing up, they either had no male role models to pattern their lives after, or else the role models that they did have were not walking with Christ. As a young man, what I saw, even in the church, were men dominating and beating and verbally abusing their wives--calling them names. My examples were not good. Even the world knows that it is not a good example for a young man to see women beaten by other men. I have seen men knock women to the ground and feel good about it. The women would get up wipe themselves off and run off down the street. I know now that that was not right. You see, my wife does not know how much I love her. She really does not know. You can call it growing up--or maturity. You can call it whatever you want. The bottom line is that I found the truth.

I found out who I am. Regardless of who my biological
father was, and despite the fact that I never knew
him, I am not who I am because of him. I am who
I am because of God. So I love my wife. I love her
and my children. She is the wife of my youth. God
has said, "Hold on tight to that woman that you've
married. She is the wife of your youth. Don't leave
her just because she gets a few wrinkles, or her figure
eight becomes a figure zero. Love her." Men, I'm
telling you that this is when you know that God is
doing something in you and in your marriage, when
you love your wife no matter what. You do not care
if she can never again make love to you, because
that is not what you live for. You love her. I am so
glad that the relationship that my wife and I have is
not based on sex. I allowed God to place something
within me so that I would never be ashamed of her.
I will never be ashamed to walk down the middle of
a shopping mall with her. I will never displease her by
wandering eyes, looking at another woman. Never!
Because I love her. And it is because I have been
repositioned by God and I know who I am.

# 2

# Steps To Being Repositioned

I know the struggles that men have in their personal lives outside of their families. I can identify with the burdens that many of them carry. At times they feel like a failure, trying in some way to feel good about themselves, especially if they are Christians and divorced. You see, I am a pastor who experienced divorced. I can not write this book and make someone feel that everything will be fine after a divorce. When you see for yourself the devastation that strikes your family after a divorce, you have to accept the responsibility that most of what happened is because of the absence of leadership of the man--the father.

All the days of my life will I have to live with the memory of the insurrection in my own home. Just as King David was punished with insurrection in his household as a result of his adultery with Bathsheba, so will many of us have to live out the rest of our days with the results of our sins. God forgives sin and completely blots it out, but the results linger. We can be glad that the grace of God comes in and gives us a fresh start, and then we can return to our children and break the curse off of their lives.

I know that a man goes through things that he will never talk about. It hurts to even think about all the bad choices and mistakes that have been made through the years. But I also know that men wish that they had a way to start over again. There is a way, and I would like to expose it to you.

There are five steps to being repositioned by God, to being able to start over and regain your position as a man. The first step is to come to God with all of your apprehensions, fears, disappointments, failures and sins. Gather them all together and share them with God, alone. Do not think that He is hearing your secrets for the first time, because he is not. He has known them since conception, but He has never judged you for them. It was your own heart that condemned you. God extends His grace to you. And when you talk to God, do not talk in some cold, impersonal theological terminology, but in the same manner that you talk to yourself when you are really hurting. When you do this, God will give you peace of mind and the strength to face whatever happens.

The second step is simple. Ask God to forgive you of your anger and distrust towards Him. Admit, that, by yourself, you can not handle the load of being husband, father, provider, counselor, friend and man, but that you desperately need God's help. Do not be afraid to be broken, because that is when God will gather the pieces of your life together and recreate a new man.

The third step is a little more difficult than the first two, because it requires that you expose all the hidden parts of your life to the light. Let me first tell you a story about when I was a young boy. As a child, I did not go to church regularly, because my parents were not born again nor regular churchgoers. In fact, they indulged in all kinds of sinful activities. But today, thank God, they are both saved. I picked up the ugly habit of smoking early in my teen years. My parents were not aware of this. One of my brothers, (who is two years older than I am), would always threaten to tell my parents that I smoked if I did not do certain things for him. I was hooked on tobacco, and my brother knew that as long as this part of my life was kept in the dark he had something to hold over my head. He would make me give him money and do his chores such as washing the dishes. But one day I got tired of being manipulated. I knew that the only way for me to really be free was to bring my situation out of the darkness and into the light. When I made the decision that my brother would never again be able to manipulate me with threats, I exposed myself, I became truly free.

The devil loves to torture people, and especially Christians, with the things that are hidden in their lives. We can not give the devil anything to work with in the darkness. I do not smoke anymore, because God delivered me from it, but I did discover a truth that will be with me for a lifetime. That truth is this: Satan's negatives are developed in the darkness. Let the light of God shine on the hidden parts of your life, and Satan will have no way to exploit them.

The last two steps to being repositioned are these: Tell your wife that, with the help of God, you will never again offend her, but will always defend her. Do not say that you will try to do this, because that gives you an out, an excuse not to live up to your word. Give her your word, and keep it. Finally, bless your children by being with them and telling them how much you love them. Be their hero by pointing them to your hero, Jesus Christ. No longer try to make yourself out to be something that you are not. Be yourself, then you will not have to try to keep up an image that you just can not maintain.

God is your strength, and the responsibilities that you have are all performed by the strength of God residing inside of you.

# 3

# Who Am I

Who am I? Have you ever asked yourself this question? As a born again Christian, you need never ask this question again, because by the time that you finish reading this you should be fully aware of who you are.

We sometimes think of ourselves as nothing. Others might think the same. This may, in part, be true if we do not have Jesus Christ in our lives. But none of this is really important in the greater scheme of things. What is important is what God thinks and says about us--what He says about me. What God's Word says is that I am not who I think I am. I am not who others think I am. I am whatever God says that I am.

## I am the righteousness of God.

Even though I might sometimes think of myself as not being righteous, God's Word says in II Corinthians 5:21 that through Jesus Christ my sins are forgiven and forgotten by God and I am "made the righteousness of God in Him." Though others, and even I, myself, have the constant remembrance of my past sins, God places those sins in "the sea of forgetfulness" and "remembers them not". Once I have accepted Jesus Christ as my personal savior, I am considered the righteousness of God through Him. This means that I am approved and acceptable and in right standing with God by His goodness.

## I am worth God's greatest sacrifice.

John 3:16 says that "...God so loved the world, that He gave His only begotten Son, that whosoever believeth in Him should not perish but have everlasting life." God so dearly prized my soul that He gave His only begotten Son for me! It is not that I am worthy of such a sacrifice, because the Bible tells us that "...all have sinned and come short of the glory of God", and that "...the wages of sin is death."

Yet because God loved me so, He purchased my salvation with the blood of His Son, Jesus.

I may not have been worthy of God's greatest sacrifice, but His Son's death on the cross proves that I am certainly <u>worth</u> it.

## I am Lord of His creation.

Psalms 8:4-8 tells me that I was created to control and subdue this earth. The sixth verse says, "Thou madest him [me] to have dominion over the works of Thy hands; Thou hast put all things under his [my] feet." God has entrusted me with the responsibility for this planet. I am actually the ruler of the earth. All things are placed under my feet (my control)--even Satan. It is time that I and my brothers and sisters in Christ take our rightful place in creation and become true lords of this earth.

## I am God's son.

I was created in God's image, and He has bestowed upon me the title of "Son of God". I John 3:1 says, "Behold what manner of love the Father hath bestowed upon us, that we should be called the Sons of God." I am not biologically the Son of God as Jesus Christ is, but I am adopted by the Father (Romans 8:15). When I was given birth by my mother, I was born of corruptible seed, but when I received Jesus Christ into my life, I was born again of incorruptible seed, as stated in I Peter 1:23. John 1:12 says, "But as many as received Him (Jesus), to them gave He power to become the Sons of God...".

The Devil would enjoy nothing more than to cause me to deny my sonship with the Father and keep me down and in a depressed state, because he knows that if I come to realize not only who I am but whose I am, I will be exalted above the dark clouds he tries to place in my life and will begin to manifest my authority, power, privilege and rights as a Child of God.

## I am more than a Conqueror.

In Romans 8:37, Paul gives a very powerful, strong, confident and uplifting reply to the preceeding verses which ask the question, "Who shall separate us from the love of Christ?" Paul says that we are "more than conquerors through Him that loved us." I don't think that he was talking about physically conquering by dint of hard effort, because Paul knew that alone he was no conqueror. The phrase "more that conquerors" is taken from the Greek word "hupernikao", which is made up of the two words, "nikao", which means "to conquer, to carry off the victory, to come away victorious", and "huper" which means "above" Thus the word "hupernikao" means to come off more than victorious; to gain a surpassing victory; to be more than a conqueror.

Paul knew personally what it was like coming off the battlefield without a victory. The Bible tells us that he was being troubled by a messenger of Satan who caused a physical affliction in his body. Three times Paul asked the Lord to take away his affliction. But instead, Jesus made a statement that turned Paul's stumbling blocks, failures and afflictions into a staircase leading up to greater dimensions of spiritual victory. Jesus said, "My grace is sufficient for thee; for my strength is made perfect in weakness" (II Corinthians 12:7-10). Jesus was telling Paul that it is not through our own power that we are able to come out on top, because our human resources are no match for the powers of darkness. But through the power of Jesus in us we are able to overcome all things. When we have done all that we are humanly able and fall on our faces and ask God's help with our problems, then we become truly aware and appreciative of His awesome power. We should stop trying to handle our problems alone, because we will always stare failures in the face until we understand the words of Paul inspired by the Holy Spirit, that

"...we are more than conquerors <u>through Him</u> (Jesus) that loved us." Too many times we are faced with anxieties, perplexities, trials, tests, family problems, financial difficulties, rejections, etc., and we feel as if we can not go on. Sometimes we just want to throw in the towel and give up. When it comes to that point, we should not look behind us or to our left or right, but look our problems in the face and refuse to be defeated. God knows us better than we know ourselves, and if He says that we are more than conquerors and can overcome all things, we have to know that no matter what we face we can not be defeated if we stand on God's promises.

## I am greater than the angels.

To some, this is a controversial statement. How, they ask, are we greater than the angels? How can I make such a statement? Is it biblical? Am I sincerely stating a biblical truth when I say this, or simply being vain?

You must first understand that I am not saying that I am <u>better</u> than the angels, but that I am <u>greater</u>

than they are. To be better is to exceed another in some effort or to be of a higher quality in some measurable aspect. This is not what I am referring to at all. When I say that I am greater than the angels, I am speaking in terms of office or position. To fully understand what I mean one must first understand that man exists simultaneously on three different levels or dimensions. The three-fold nature of man is that he is spirit, soul and body (read I Thessalonians 5:23). The body is physical; the soul is mental, intellectual and emotional; the spirit is the essence of God which animates the body and sparks the intellect. It is in the spirit realm that I am greater than the angels. Through Jesus Christ, I am made a "Son of God" (see above). Because I am a son of God, I am heir to all the rights and privileges of my Father, who is Lord of all. Angels, on the other hand, are spirit beings created by God as His servants in the spirit realm. If they are servants of the Father, then they are also servants of His children. They are my servants, because I am one of God's children. I am a Son of the most high God. Angels are not sons. They were created by God to perform certain specific tasks. One of those tasks is to watch over me (Psalms 34:7 and II Kings 6:8-17). While Jesus was here on earth, he understood the role of the angels with respect to Him. Physically, He was less than the angels, but spiritually He was God. After the Devil had tempted Him in the wilderness, the Bible tells us that the angels came to minister to [serve] Him (John 4:1-11). In Matthew 26:53, Jesus asked Peter, "Thinkest thou that I cannot now pray to my Father, and He shall presently give me more than twelve legions of angels."

## I am created in His image.

Genesis 1:26 says, "...and God said, Let us make man in our image, after our likeness...". I do not think that He was talking of making us in His physical image, to look like Him, because God is not physical. God is spirit (John 4:24). When God created man, He made our spirit just like His. He gave us dominion, the capacity of conscious thought and free will just as He has. Spiritually, Adam was essentially as God until he sinned. His spirit was then stained by that sin, but it still contained in it the essence of God and the potential to be reconciled to God. That same spirit resides in me because even though God only created the first man, Adam, and then the first woman, Eve, He gave them the ability to reproduce after their own kind. So the same spirit, the essence and likeness of God that was placed in them, was passed on by them to their children. And through them that spirit has passed to me. Therefore, I am created in <u>His image</u>. Just as God was able to speak creation into existence (Genesis 1) through His spirit residing in me, there is power in the words I speak in the name of Jesus. I thank God for Him being my spiritual Father, and like any good son, I want to be just like Him. The more that I read the Bible and understand how God is, the better I understand myself and how I am to live my life.

## I am forgiven.

As was stated earlier, the Bible tells us that all have sinned and come short of God's glory. Of all the billions who have lived on this earth, only Jesus was able to live a blameless, spotless and sinless life. When He gave His life on the cross, it was not in payment for His own sins, because He had none. Instead, He was able to take the sins of the world onto Himself and pay for them with His own blood. His death paid the ransom for all our sins so that we might be forgiven. It mattered not whether I was a liar, thief, murderer, drunk, junkie, wife beater, homosexual, adulterer, rapist or simply someone who likes dirty movies. When I asked God for forgiveness, my whole slate was wiped clean by the blood of Jesus. Hebrews 10:17 says, "And their sins and iniquities will I [God] remember no more." God forgives and forgets all our transgressions. There is no record, film or memory in heaven of my past. When the Devil tries to remind me of my past sins, I can say, "What sins are you talking about. Those don't exist anymore, because God has forgiven me of them." (Ephesians 4:32, Colossians 2:13, James 5:15, I John 2:12)

## I am His Ambassador on Earth

The word "ambassador" is defined as "A diplomatic official of the highest rank. A person set by one sovereign or state to another as its resident representative." An ambassador carries a lot of responsibility. His job is to establish, maintain or better the relationship between the nation or king that sent him and the nation or king to which he is sent. In the natural world, the job of ambassador is a very important one.

II Corinthians 5:20 says, "Now then we are ambassadors for Christ, as though God did beseech you by us: we pray you in Christ's stead, be ye reconciled to God." As an ambassador of Christ, I am to reconcile others back to the father. I am to help others see the Light of Christ, repent of their sins and be born again. Just as earthly ambassadors are dispatched to foreign lands to dwell among a strange people, so am I dwelling in a strange land among a people who are not as I am. I belong to a higher city. But I am dispatched to dwell among sinners so that I might tell them of the glory of the kingdom to which I belong. I am on a mission to bring as many as will come into the glorious light of that kingdom and of its prince, who is the Christ. The eternal future of all the population of the Earth depends on how well I and my fellow ambassadors fulfill our mission.

In the natural world, an ambassador is supported materially by the country that he represents. They provide him a place to live and work, and give him privileges, pay and benefits commensurate with his high position. In retirement he is taken care of because of the service that he has given. As God's ambassador I am provided for by the Father. As long as I do my job, my every need <u>and desire</u> is met through Christ. And the retirement benefits are out of this world (literally). Some may try to tell me that I am not important because I am not a minister or a deacon, but I know that as God's ambassador on Earth, mine is the most important job in the kingdom. Even if all I do is sweep the floors of the church everyday, if I am faithful in witnessing to the lost, when my time is done I will be recalled to my home city, which is in the presence of God, and His Son, Jesus.

## I am a citizen of Heaven.

A citizen is a native or naturalized member of a state or nation who owes allegiance to its government and is entitled to its protection. Paul writes in Ephesians 2:19, "Now therefore ye are no more strangers and foreigners, but fellow-citizens with the saints and of the household of God." Before I became a citizen of the kingdom of God, I was a stranger to God's people, and a foreigner to His nation. The word "stranger is from the Greek "zenos", which means "alien". The word speaks of that which is a different quality or nature than something else, thus alien to it. Sinners are aliens to the kingdom of God, having a totally depraved nature that makes them different in a hostile sense. The Greek word translated in the scripture as "foreigners" is "paraoikos", which consists of "para" (alongside) and "oikeo" (to make one's home). The sense given here is of one who comes from one country or city and settles in another, but does not become a citizen. Though in the beginning I was a citizen of the world and a stranger to the kingdom of God, once I accepted Christ and became a citizen of the kingdom (John 1:13), I became a stranger and a foreigner in the world. As a born-again believer, this world is not my home. I am in the world, but I am no longer of it. In His prayer for all believers in John 17:14 Jesus said, "...they are not of the world even as I [Christ] am not of the world." The household of God mentioned in Ephesians 2:19 is not a household here on the Earth. The household of God is with God in His kingdom. My true citizenship is in heaven with my Lord Jesus Christ.

In praying to the Father in John 17:15, Jesus said, "I pray not that Thou shouldest take them out of the world, but that Thou shouldest keep them from the evil." In the 18th verse of the same chapter, He said, "As Thou hast sent me into the world, even so I also have sent them into the world." Even though I am no longer a citizen of this world, Jesus wants me to remain in the world to continue and complete the job that He started. I am to win souls to Christ and reconcile the world to the Father. All who accept

Christ as savior and Lord are strangers passing through this world. So I say this to the reader: While passing through this world, if there is any kind deed you can do or encouraging word that you can give, do it, for you may not pass this way again. When things do not go as you would wish, remember where your mansion is. Do not get discouraged or become worried, for Christ will continue to supply your every need according to His riches in glory. Continue to store up your treasures in Heaven (your real home) where moth or rust cannot corrupt.

## I am saved.

The unsaved often ask Christians, "How does one become saved?" In response, many Christians give answers from their own experiences instead of from the Bible. In a recent survey, six out of ten people who call themselves Christians could not give a biblical answer to this question. Why not? It is clear that the six so-called Christians were not too concerned with reading and studying the Bible. I Peter 3:15 says that we should "...be ready always to give an answer to every man that asketh you a reason of the hope that is in you..." A Christian should be not only able, but eager to give an answer for his faith whenever and wherever he is confronted, whether by the Devil or by another person. When I received Jesus Christ as savior and Lord of my life, I was immediately attacked by Satan. He told me that I was not saved, that I had not done anything to deserve salvation, that I was a sinner, that I was too bad to be saved, and even went so far as to tell me that I was the Anti-Christ. If I had listened to what I was told at that time and had not known for sure that I was saved, I probably would not be saved today. Ephesians 2:8 says, "For by grace are ye saved through faith; and that not of yourselves; it is the gift of God." Because I knew this particular verse, I knew why I was saved. So every time the Devil threw a negative at me, I countered with a positive. I told him that I was saved by grace through faith. Though I did not deserve to be saved, God's grace--His unmerited favor and abundant mercy--working through my faith was able to save me.

There are times when the Devil tries to persuade us to be ashamed of being saved. He tries to put blinders over our eyes so that we cannot see the truth. He tells us that we are outnumbered by the unsaved, that we are the only Christians on our jobs, that we are the only ones trying to live a saved life. If we allow ourselves to succomb to Satan's negative thoughts, the results are negative results such as depression, discouragement and dismay. This is exactly what happened to one of the greatest prophets of old, Elijah. We can find the story in the 19th chapter of I Kings.

> And Ahab told Jezebel all that Elijah had done, and withal how he had slain all the prophets with the sword. Then Jezebel sent a messenger unto Elijah saying, so let the Gods do to me, and more also, if I make not thy life as the life of one of them by tomorrow about this time. And when he saw that, he arose, and went for his life, and came to Beersheba, which belongeth to Judah, and left his servant there. (Verses 1-3)
> And he came thither unto a cave and lodged there; and behold, the word of the Lord came to him, and He said unto him, What doest thou here, Elijah? And he said I have been very jealous for the Lord God of hosts; for the children of Israel have forsaken thy covenant, thrown down thine altars, and slain thy prophets with the sword; and I, even I only, am left; and they seek my life to take it away. (Verses 9-10)

To this, God replied that Elijah had nothing to fear, because even though all those things had happened, "Yet I have left me seven thousand in Israel, all the knees which have not bowed to Baal, and every mouth which hath not kissed him." (Verse 18)

So when the Devil comes at me with his negative talk, and even though it may seem that I am the last Christian on the Earth (though I know that I am not) I will never be ashamed to proclaim that Christ is Lord, for greater is He that is in me than he that is in the world. Though I was blind, now I see; though lost, I am found. Through the blood of Jesus Christ, **I AM SAVED AND REPOSITIONED FOR GREATNESS.**

## Audio Cassette Offer

MB 245

**The Principle of Good and Evil** - Since we know that we are creatures capable of sinning; is there a possibility that evil will always triumph over good? The good news is no! This series expands on the nature of both good and evil and how you, the believer, can walk in the nature of God which is His goodness.
**2-cassette audio series: $13.00**

MB 244

**The Presence Of Curses** - The sin of the father will often attempt to visit this present generation... however, those who understand their authority in Christ can refuse that visitation!!
This series reveals the methods of identifying curses that attempt to reduplicate themselves generation after generation.
**2-cassette audio series: $13.00**

MB 408

**How To Have A Victorious Marriage** - Marriages are breaking up at such a fast rate that 90% of the attorneys today now handle divorce cases. No one person got married and knew how to be a good spouse. Achieving "good spouse" status comes as a result of trial and error. But to discover effectiveness in a marital relationship comes from the Source that designed it.
This is a teaching on how-to according to God's Word.
**4-cassette audio series: $21.00**

# Mail Order

To order additional copies of **God's Repositioned Man**, complete the information below.

Ship to: (please print)

Name _____

Address _____

City, State, Zip _____

Day phone _____


_____ copies of *God's Repositioned Man* @ $8.95 each  $ _____
(*Postage and handling are included with the price*)


_____ copies & title _____  $ _____

of teaching cassette series.


If you live outside the USA please add an additional  $ __2.00__

Total amount enclosed  $ _____

Make checks payable to: **Christian Joy Center**

Send to: *Christian Joy Center • 1208 Sumac Dr. • El Paso, TX. 79925*

*(915) 595-1307 or fax (915) 595-1493*

-------------------------------------------------------------

## Teaching Cassettes Orders

• Pricing on all teaching series include the price of shipping and handling.

• For more information write or call the above address or telephone number.